P9-DGB-393

To:

From:

Feeding
Imagination
A Nash Finch Educational Program

My Book of Devotions

A Guide for Parents & Kids

about Forgiveness

Simon & Schuster, Inc.
NEW YORK LONDON TORONTO SYDNEY

Simon & Schuster, Inc.
1230 Avenue of the Americas, New York, New York 10020

The quoted ideas expressed in this book (but not Scripture verses) are not, in all cases, exact quotations, as some have been edited for clarity and brevity. In all cases, the author has attempted to maintain the speaker's original intent. In some cases, quoted material for this book was obtained from secondary sources, primarily print media. While every effort was made to ensure the accuracy of these sources, the accuracy cannot be guaranteed. For additions, deletions, corrections, or clarifications in future editions of this text, please write Freeman-Smith, LLC.

Cover Design by Kim Russell / Wahoo Designs
Page Layout by Bart Dawson

Manufactured in the United States of America

10 9 8 7 6 5 4 3 2

ISBN-13: 978-1-4169-1576-8
ISBN-10: 1-4169-1576-1

My Book of Devotions

A Guide for Parents & Kids

about Forgiveness

For God so loved the world,
that he gave his only begotten Son,
that whosoever believeth in him
should not perish, but have
everlasting life.

John 3:16 KJV

Table of Contents

A Message to Parents

Perhaps your child's bookshelf is already filled with a happy and helpful assortment of good books for kids. If so, congratulations—that means you're a thoughtful parent who understands the importance of reading to your child. This book is intended to be an important addition to your child's library.

This little text is intended to be read by Christian parents to their young children. The book contains 31 brief chapters, one for each day of the month. Each chapter consists of a Bible verse, a brief story, kid-friendly quotations from notable Christian thinkers, a timely tip, and a prayer. Every chapter examines a different aspect of an important topic: forgiveness.

For the next 31 days, take the time to read one chapter each night to your child, and then spend a few moments talking about the chapter's meaning. By the end of the month, you will have had 31 different opportunities to share God's wisdom with your son or daughter, and that's good . . . very good.

If you have been touched by God's love and His grace, then you know the joy that He has brought into your own life. Now it's your turn to share His message with the boy or girl whom He has entrusted to your care. Happy reading! And may God richly bless you and yours.

God Wants Us to Forgive

Yes, if you forgive others for the things they do wrong, then your Father in heaven will also forgive you for the things you do wrong.

Matthew 6:14 ICB

The Bible tells us this: When other people do things that are wrong, we should forgive them. God's Word also tells us that when we're willing to forgive others, God is quick to forgive us for the mistakes that we make.

Has somebody done something that makes you angry? Talk things over with your mom or dad, and then be ready to forgive the person who has hurt your feelings. And remember: God wants you to hurry up and forgive others, just like God is always in a hurry to forgive you.

Big Idea for Kids

Making up may not be as hard as you think! If there is someone who has been unkind to you, perhaps it's time for the two of you to make up. If you're willing to be the first person to say something nice, you'll discover that making up is usually easier than you think.

Learning how to forgive and forget is
one of the secrets of a happy Christian life.
Warren Wiersbe

Big Idea for Parents

Becoming a model of forgiveness: If you want your children to learn the art of forgiveness, then you must master that art yourself. If you're able to forgive those who have hurt you and, by doing so, move on with your life, your kids will learn firsthand that forgiveness is God's way.

Today's Prayer

Dear Lord, you have forgiven me. Now, it's my turn to forgive others. Help me fill my heart with kind thoughts, and help me fill each day with good deeds. Thank you, Lord, for Your love, for Your forgiveness, and for Your Son Jesus.

Amen

Do for other people the same things
you want them to do for you.

Matthew 7:12 ICB

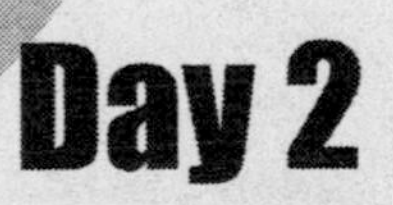

The words of Matthew 7:12 remind us that, as believers in Christ, we should treat others as we wish to be treated. This is called the Golden Rule, but for Christians, it's worth much more than gold.

Do you want other people to forgive you when you make mistakes? Of course you do. And that's why you should be willing to forgive them.

The Golden Rule should be your tool for deciding how you will treat others. So use the Golden Rule as your guide for living and forgiving!

Big Idea for Kids

When in doubt . . . talk it out! If you're uncertain about a particular situation, talk it over with your parents. They'll help you decide how to handle things in the best way. So if you have a doubt about it, talk about it . . . Now!

Forgiveness is contagious.
First you forgive them, and pretty soon,
they'll forgive you, too.

Marie T. Freeman

Big Idea for Parents

You are an example; be a good one: Your children will learn how to treat others by watching you; be kindhearted, understanding and forgiving to everyone, starting with the precious people who live under your roof.

Today's Prayer

Dear Lord, help me always to do
my very best to treat others
as I wish to be treated.
The Golden Rule is Your rule, Father;
let me also make it mine.
Amen

What It Means to Forgive

Peter said to them,
"Change your hearts and lives . . .
in the name of Jesus Christ."
Acts 2:38 NCV

What does it mean to forgive? Forgiveness means that you decide to change your angry thoughts into kind thoughts. Forgiveness means that you decide not to stay mad at somebody who has done something wrong. Forgiveness happens when you decide that obeying God is more important than staying angry.

Sometimes forgiveness can be very hard, but it's the right thing to do. Why? Because forgiveness is God's way, and you should make it your way, too!

Big Idea for Kids

The next time you're standing in line, don't try to push ahead of your neighbors. After all, if you don't want other people breaking in line in front of you, then you shouldn't break in line in front of them!

Forgiveness is God's command.
Martin Luther

Big Idea for Parents

Holding a grudge? Drop it! How can you expect your kids to forgive others if you don't? Never expect your children to be more forgiving than you are.

Today's Prayer

Dear Lord, today, I am going to forgive others. When I forgive other people, I know that I am obeying your instructions. And I know that I am also getting rid of angry feelings that can hurt me more than they hurt anybody else. So today, I will forgive and keep forgiving, just like You always forgive me. Amen

Forgive and Forget?

He has taken our sins away from us as far as the east is from west.

Psalm 103:12 ICB

Have you heard the saying, "Forgive and forget"? Well, it's certainly easier said than done. It's easy to talk about forgiving somebody, but actually forgiving that person can be much harder to do. And when it comes to forgetting, forget about it!

Sometimes, it's impossible to forget the people who hurt our feelings. But even if we can't forget, we can forgive. And that's exactly what God teaches us to do.

Big Idea for Kids

What's good for you is good for them, too: If you want others to try their best to "forgive and forget" your mistakes, then you should do the same for them.

God forgets the past. Imitate him.

Max Lucado

Big Idea for Parents

Help from the sidelines: As parents, we can't make our children forgive others, but we can coach them on the art of forgiveness. All of us, whether youngsters or grown-ups, learn the art of forgiveness when we learn to treat others as we wish to be treated. And if that sounds suspiciously like the Golden Rule, that's because it is the Golden Rule.

Today's Prayer

Dear Lord, it's so easy to judge
other people, but it's also easy to
misjudge them. Only You can judge
a human heart, Lord, so let me love
my friends and let me forgive them
when they make mistakes, but never
let me make the mistake of
judging them; instead,
I'll leave judging up to You.
Amen

When We're Angry

A wise person is patient.
He will be honored if he ignores
a wrong done against him.
Proverbs 19:11 ICB

When you're angry, you will be tempted to say things and do things that you'll regret later. But don't do them! Instead of doing things in a hurry, slow down long enough to calm yourself down.

Jesus does not intend that you strike out against other people, and He doesn't intend that your heart be troubled by anger. Your heart should instead be filled with love, just like Jesus' heart was . . . and is!

Big Idea for Kids

Time Out!: If you become angry, slow yourself down before you say unkind words or do unkind things—not after. It's perfectly okay to place yourself in "time out" until you can calm down.

Life is too short to spend it
being angry, bored, or dull.
Barbara Johnson

Big Idea for Parents

Don't fan the flames: When your children become angry or upset, you'll tend to become angry and upset, too. Resist that temptation. As the grown-up person in the family, it's up to you to remain calm, even when other, less mature members of the family, can't.

Today's Prayer

Dear Lord, I can be so impatient,
and I can become so angry.
Calm me down, Lord, and help me to be
a patient, forgiving Christian. Just as
You have forgiven me, Father, let me
forgive others so that I can follow
the example of Your Son.
Amen

Forgiving Friends

It is good and pleasant when
God's people live together in peace!
Psalm 133:1 NCV

The Bible tells us that friendship can be a wonderful thing. That's why it's good to know how to make and to keep good friends. And one way that we keep friends is to forgive them when they make mistakes.

If you want to make lots of friends, practice the Golden Rule with everybody you know. Be kind. Share. Say nice things. Be quick to forgive, and be helpful. When you do, you'll discover that the Golden Rule isn't just a nice way to behave; it's also a great way to make and to keep friends!

Big Idea for Kids

Everybody is a VIP: VIP means "Very Important Person." To God, everybody is a VIP, and we should treat every person with dignity, patience, and respect.

Forget the faults of others
by remembering your own.
John Bunyan

Big Idea for Parents

It takes time and understanding! Sometimes our children are impatient to build friendships. Make sure that your child understands that it takes time, effort, and understanding to build friendships that last.

Today's Prayer

Dear Lord, when somebody hurts
my feelings, let me be patient
and kind. And when a friend does
something wrong, help me do the right
thing by offering my forgiveness
sooner rather than later!
Amen

When Forgiveness Is Hard

I tell you, love your enemies.
Pray for those who hurt you.
If you do this, you will be true sons
of your Father in heaven.
Matthew 6:44-45 ICB

Is forgiving someone else an easy thing for you to do or a hard thing? If you're like most people, forgiving others can be hard, Hard, HARD! But even if you're having a very hard time forgiving someone, you can do it if you talk things over with your parents, and if you talk things over with God.

Big Idea for Kids

If you're having trouble forgiving someone else . . . think how many times other people have forgiven you!

When God forgives, He forgets. He buries our sins in the sea and puts a sign on the shore saying, "No Fishing Allowed." Let's forgive other people in the very same way.

Corrie ten Boom

Big Idea for Parents

If it were easy: If forgiveness were easy, everybody would be doing it. But, of course, forgiveness can, at times, be a very hard thing to do. So be quick to explain to your child that forgiving another person—even when it's difficult—is the correct thing to do.

Today's Prayer

Dear Lord, even when forgiveness
is hard, help me be a person
who forgives other people,
just as You have forgiven me.
Amen

Learning to Be Patient

Always be humble and gentle.
Be patient and accept each other with love.
Ephesians 4:2 ICB

Jesus teaches us the Golden Rule for living: We should treat other people in the same way that we want to be treated. And because we want other people to be patient with us, we, in turn, must be patient with them.

Being patient with other people means treating them with kindness, respect, and understanding. It means forgiving our friends when they've done something we don't like. Sometimes, it's hard to be patient, but we've got to do our best. And when we do, we're following the Golden Rule—God's rule for how to treat others—and everybody wins!

Big Idea for Kids

It's your turn . . . God and your parents have been patient with you . . . now it's your turn to be patient with others.

No matter what we are going through,
no matter how long the waiting for answers,
of one thing we may be sure.
God is faithful. He keeps His promises.
What he starts, He finishes . . .
including His perfect work in us.
Gloria Gaither

Big Idea for Parents

Imitating Him while imitating you: Kids imitate their parents, so act accordingly! The best way for your children to learn how to follow in Christ's footsteps is by following you while you follow Him!

Today's Prayer

Dear Lord, sometimes it's hard to be
patient, and that's exactly when
I should try my hardest to be patient.
Help me to obey You by being a patient,
loving person . . . even when it's hard.
Amen

Asking for Forgiveness

But if we confess our sins, he will forgive our sins, because we can trust God to do what is right. He will cleanse us from all the wrongs we have done.

1 John 1:9 NCV

When you make a mistake or hurt someone's feelings, what should you do? You should say you're sorry and ask for forgiveness. And you should do so sooner, not later.

The longer you wait to apologize, the harder it is on you. So if you've done something wrong, don't be afraid to ask for forgiveness, and don't be afraid to ask for it NOW!

Big Idea for Kids

Sorry you said it? Apologize! Did you say something that hurt someone's feelings? Then it's time for an apology: yours. It's never too late to apologize, but it's never too early, either!

God sees everything we've ever done
and He's willing to forgive.
But we must confess to him.
Ruth Bell Graham

Big Idea for Parents

When it's over, it's over . . . When your child sincerely apologizes and makes amends, then it's time for you, as the parent, to demonstrate the art of forgiveness—and the art of creative forgetfulness—by accepting your child's apology and moving on.

Today's Prayer

Dear Lord, when I make mistakes,
I will admit what I've done, and I will
apologize to the people I've hurt.
You are perfect, Lord; I am not.
I thank You for Your forgiveness
and for Your love.
Amen

From the Heart

Create in me a pure heart,
God, and make my spirit right again.
Psalm 51:10 NCV

Where does forgiveness start? It starts in our hearts and works its way out from there. Jesus taught us that a pure heart is a wonderful blessing. It's up to each of us to fill our hearts with love for God, love for Jesus, and love for all people. When we do, we are blessed.

Do you want to be the best person you can be? Then invite the love of Christ into your heart and share His love with your family and friends. And remember that lasting love always comes from a pure heart . . . like yours!

Big Idea for Kids

Show them how you feel: It's good to tell your loved ones how you feel about them, but that's not enough. You should also show them how you feel with your good deeds and your kind words.

Let us learn to cast our hearts into God.

St. Bernard of Clairvaux

Big Idea for Parents

Learning from a heart like yours . . . Your children will learn how to treat others by watching you (not by listening to you!). Your own genuine acts of kindness and forgiveness will speak far louder than your words.

Today's Prayer

Dear Lord, You have given me the gift of love; let me share that gift with others today and every day.

Amen

Don't Be Cruel

A kind person is doing himself a favor.
But a cruel person brings
trouble upon himself.
Proverbs 11:17 ICB

Day 11

Sometimes, young people can be very mean. They may make fun of other people, and when they do so, it's wrong. Period.

As Christians, we should be kind to everyone. And, if other kids say unkind things to a child or make fun of him or her, it's up to us to step in and lend a helping hand.

Today and every day, be a person who is known for your kindness, not for your cruelty. That's how God wants you to behave. Period.

Big Idea for Kids

Don't be cruel: Sometimes, you can be too honest, especially if you say unkind things that are intended to hurt other people's feelings. When you're deciding what to say, you should mix honesty and courtesy together. When you do, you'll say the right thing.

Brotherly love is still the distinguishing badge of every true Christian.

Matthew Henry

Big Idea for Parents

Play Fair: Never try to win an argument by hurting another person; it's simply not worth it. Besides, your kids are probably watching.

Today's Prayer

Dear Lord, sometimes people are cruel. Let me never be such a person. Let me treat others as I wish to be treated, and let my thoughts and actions honor You today and forever.

Amen

Playing by the Rules: God's Rules

But the truly happy person is the one who carefully studies God's perfect law that makes people free. He continues to study it. He listens to God's teaching and does not forget what he heard. Then he obeys what God's teaching says. When he does this, it makes him happy.

James 1:25 ICB

Day 12

We know that it's right to forgive other people and wrong to stay angry with them. But sometimes, it's so much easier to do the wrong thing than it is to do the right thing, especially when we're tired or frustrated.

When you do the right thing by forgiving other people, you'll feel good because you'll know that you're obeying God. And that's a very good feeling indeed. So make this promise to yourself and keep it: play by the rules—God's rules. You'll always be glad you did.

Big Idea for Kids

Even if you're a very good person, you shouldn't expect to be happy all the time. Sometimes, things will happen to make you sad, and it's okay to be sad when bad things happen to you. But remember: through good times and bad, you'll always be happier if you obey the rules of your Father in heaven. So obey them!

> Rules were created not to spoil your fun but to protect and provide for you.
>
> Charles Stanley

Big Idea for Parents

Logical Consequences! The world won't protect your child from the consequences of misbehavior, and neither should you. As a parent, your job is to ensure that the consequences of your child's actions are logical, measured, appropriate, and thoroughly understood by your youngster.

Today's Prayer

Dear Lord, Your laws are right for me;
let me live by those laws.
And, let me be a good example for
others so that they, too, might follow
in the footsteps of Your Son Jesus.
Amen

Teaching Others by Example

You are young, but do not let anyone treat you as if you were not important. Be an example to show the believers how they should live. Show them with your words, with the way you live, with your love, with your faith, and with your pure life.

1 Timothy 4:12 ICB

What kind of example are you? Are you the kind of person who shows other people what it means to be kind and forgiving? Hopefully so!!!

How hard is it to say a kind word? Not very! How hard is it to accept someone's apology? Usually not too hard. So today, be a good example for others to follow. Because God needs people, like you, who are willing to stand up and be counted for Him. And that's exactly the kind of example you should try to be.

Big Idea for Kids

Cheerfulness by example. Do you need a little cheering up? If so, find somebody else who needs cheering up, too. Then, do your best to brighten that person's day. When you do, you'll discover that cheering up other people is a wonderful way to cheer yourself up, too!

More depends on my walk than my talk.
D. L. Moody

Big Idea for Parents

Your life is a sermon: preach and teach accordingly: The sermons you live are far more important than the ones you preach. Make no mistake, your kids are watching carefully and learning constantly.

Today's Prayer

Dear Lord, You have wonderful plans for me, and You know the kind of person You want me to become. Let me be that kind of person. And let me be the right kind of example for my friends and family—today and every day.
Amen

Mistakes Happen . . . to Everybody

I waited patiently for the Lord,
He turned to me and heard my cry . . .
He made my feet steady.

Psalm 40:1-2 ICB

When other people make mistakes, you must find a way to forgive them. And when you make mistakes, as you will from time to time, you must hope that other people will forgive you, too.

When you have done things that you regret, you should apologize, you should clean up the mess you've made, you should learn from your mistakes, and—last but not least—you should forgive yourself. Mistakes happen . . . it's simply a fact of life, and it's simply a part of growing up. So don't be too hard on yourself, especially if you've learned something along the way.

Big Idea for Kids

When other people have made a mistake . . . it's a mistake not to forgive them.

God is able to take mistakes and make something good out of them—something for our good and for His glory.

Ruth Bell Graham

Big Idea for Parents

When you fall short, ask for forgiveness: Nobody's perfect; no, not even you. When you make mistakes, as you most certainly will from time to time, ask for forgiveness, especially if you're seeking it from your kids. Your behavior will serve as a priceless example to your children.

Today's Prayer

Dear Lord, sometimes I make mistakes.
When I do, forgive me, Father.
And help me learn from my mistakes
so that I can be a better servant to
You and a better example to
my friends and family.
Amen

Get Over It!

Brothers and sisters, I know that I have not yet reached that goal, but there is one thing I always do. Forgetting the past and straining toward what is ahead, I keep trying to reach the goal and get the prize for which God called me through Christ to the life above.

Philippians 3:13-14 NCV

Day 15

An important part of learning how to forgive is learning how to get over the things that happened yesterday. What happened yesterday is past. And, if what happened yesterday has made you unhappy, today is as good a day as any to start getting over your hurt feelings.

Are you still angry with someone? Has that person said he was sorry and tried to make things better? If so, talk to your parents about it! They'll help you understand that you can't change the past, but you can get over it.

Big Idea for Kids

Tempted to fight? Walk away. The best fights are those that never happen.

No matter what,
don't ever let yesterday use up
too much of today.
Barbara Johnson

Big Idea for Parents

Discuss the Importance of Forgiveness: Teach the importance of forgiveness every day and, if necessary, use words.

Today's Prayer

Dear Lord, let me learn from what happened yesterday, but don't let me stay angry about what happened yesterday. Let me forgive others just as You have forgiven me, and let me be a happy, cheerful person today and every day.

Amen

How Often Should We Forgive?

Then Peter came to Jesus and asked, "Lord, when my fellow believer sins against me, how many times must I forgive him? Should I forgive him as many as seven times?" Jesus answered, "I tell you, you must forgive him more than seven times. You must forgive him even if he does wrong to you seventy-seven times."

Matthew 18:21-22 NCV

If you forgive somebody once, that's enough, right? WRONG!!! Even if you've forgiven somebody many times before, you must keep on forgiving.

Jesus teaches us that we must keep forgiving people even if they continue to misbehave. Why? Because we, too, need to be forgiven over and over again. And if God keeps forgiving us, then we must be willing to do the same thing for others.

Big Idea for Kids

Forgive . . . and keep forgiving! Sometimes, you may forgive someone once and then, at a later time, become angry at the very same person again. If so, you must forgive that person again and again . . . until it sticks!

> How often should you forgive the other person? Only as many times as you want God to forgive you!
>
> Marie T. Freeman

Big Idea for Parents

It starts at home . . . and as the parent, you're in charge of demonstrating the fine art of forgiveness. It's a big job, so don't be afraid to ask for help . . . especially God's help.

Today's Prayer

Dear Lord, thank You for loving me and forgiving me. I will return Your love by sharing it . . . today and every day.

Amen

When We're Tired

The Lord gives strength
to those who are tired.
Isaiah 40:29 ICB

Some rules are easier to understand than they are to live by. Jesus told us that we should treat other people in the same way that we would want to be treated: that's the Golden Rule. But sometimes, especially when we're tired or upset, that rule is very hard to follow.

Jesus wants us to treat other people with respect, kindness, courtesy, and love. When we do, we make our families and friends happy . . . and we make our Father in heaven very proud. So if you're wondering how to treat someone else, ask the person you see every time you look into the mirror. The answer you receive will tell you exactly what to do.

Big Idea for Kids

Rest, rest, rest . . . Oftentimes, our anger is nothing more than exhaustion in disguise. When in doubt, get a good night's sleep.

He is the God of wholeness and restoration.
Stormie Omartian

Big Idea for Parents

Grown-ups need sleep, too . . . Most adults need about eight hours of sleep each night. If you're depriving yourself of much needed sleep in order to stay up and watch late night television, you've developed a bad habit. Instead, do yourself a favor: turn off the TV and go to bed.

Today's Prayer

Dear Lord, when I'm tired, give me the wisdom to do the smart thing: give me the wisdom to put my head on my pillow and rest!

Amen

Do Yourself a Favor

I pray also that you will have greater
understanding in your heart . . .
and that you will know how rich
and glorious are the blessings God
has promised his holy people.

Ephesians 1:18 NCV

When you forgive somebody else, you're actually doing yourself a favor. Why? Because when you forgive the other person, you get rid of angry feelings that can make you unhappy.

Are you still angry about something that happened yesterday, or the day before that, or the day before that? Do yourself a big favor: forgive everybody (including yourself, if necessary). When you do, you won't change what happened yesterday, but you will make today a whole lot better.

Big Idea for Kids

Do yourself another favor: Say it! If you love your brother or sister (and, of course, you do!) say so. But don't stop there: let all your family members know that you love them . . . a lot!

> Bitterness is the greatest barrier to friendship with God.
>
> Rick Warren

Big Idea for Parents

Focused on the past? If so, it's time to refocus! If you want your child to appreciate the precious present—and you do—then live there.

Today's Prayer

Lord, make me a generous and cheerful Christian. Let me be kind to those who need my encouragement, and let me share with those who need my help, today and every day.

Amen

Nobody's Perfect

For all have sinned and fall short
of the glory of God.
Romans 3:23 Holman CSB

Day 19

Do you make mistakes? Of course you do . . . everybody does. When you make a mistake, you must try your best to learn from it so that you won't make the very same mistake again. And, if you have hurt someone—or if you have disobeyed God—you must ask for forgiveness.

Remember: mistakes are a part of life, but the biggest mistake you can make is to keep making the same mistake over and over and over again.

Big Idea for Kids

Made a mistake? Ask for forgiveness. If you've broken one of God's rules, you can always ask Him for His forgiveness. And He will always give it!

> What makes a Christian a Christian is not perfection but forgiveness.
>
> Max Lucado

Big Idea for Parents

Parents aren't perfect: The perfect parent does not exist. So don't be too hard on yourself when you fall short of absolute perfection. Do your best, and trust God with the rest.

Today's Prayer

Dear Lord, thank You for loving me,
even when I make mistakes.
You forgive me, Lord, and so do
my parents. Let me learn to forgive
others so that I can treat other
people in the very same way that
I have been treated.
Amen

Practice, Practice, Practice

We say they are happy because they did not give up. You have heard about Job's patience, and you know the Lord's purpose for him in the end. You know the Lord is full of mercy and is kind.

James 5:11 NCV

Day 20

Forgiving other people requires practice and lots of it. So when it comes to forgiveness, here's something you should remember: if at first you don't succeed, don't give up!

Are you having trouble forgiving someone (or, for that matter, forgiving yourself for a mistake that you've made)? If so, remember that forgiveness isn't easy, so keep trying until you get it right . . . and if you keep trying, you can be sure that sooner or later, you will get it right.

Big Idea for Kids

You'll feel better! Forgiving other people is a good way to make yourself feel better. Why? First, when you forgive others, you know that you're obeying God, and that's a good feeling. Second, forgiveness is a great way to stop feeling angry—and that's a good feeling, too!

By perseverance the snail reached the ark.

C. H. Spurgeon

Big Idea for Parents

Parental Practice: To become practiced in the art of forgiveness, you need practice. For most of us—kids and grown-ups alike—forgiveness doesn't come naturally. Keep practicing until it does.

Today's Prayer

Dear Lord, when I have
trouble forgiving someone,
when I'm discouraged, or tired,
or angry, let me turn to You
for strength, for patience,
for wisdom, and for love.
Amen

How Would Jesus Behave?

And be kind and compassionate
to one another, forgiving one another,
just as God also forgave you in Christ.

Ephesians 4:32 Holman CSB

Day 21

It's easy to love people who have been nice to you, but it's very hard to love people who have treated you badly. Still, Jesus instructs us to treat both our friends and our enemies with kindness and respect.

Are you having problems being nice to someone? Is there someone you know whom you just don't like very much? Remember that Jesus not only forgave His enemies, but He also loved them . . . and so should you.

Big Idea for Kids

If you're not sure that it's the right thing to do, don't do it! And if you're not sure that Jesus would approve of what you're about to say, don't say it.

We have in Jesus Christ a perfect example of how to put God's truth into practice.

Bill Bright

Big Idea for Parents

It's up to us: Our children will learn about Jesus at church and, in some cases, at school. But, the ultimate responsibility for religious teachings should never be delegated to institutions outside the home. As parents, we must teach our children about the love and grace of Jesus Christ by our words and by our actions.

Today's Prayer

Dear Lord, I am a very lucky person,
and I thank You for my blessings.
Help me to be a good person,
and help me use my talents and
my possessions for Your Glory . . .
and for Your Son.
Amen

Forgiving Yourself!

The Lord says, "Forget what happened before. Do not think about the past. Look at the new thing I am going to do."

Isaiah 43:18-19 ICB

Day 22

Are you perfect? Of course not! Even if you're a very good person, you're bound to mistakes and lots of them. And when you make a mistake, you should ask for forgiveness from a very important person: yourself!

After you've made a mistake, you'll probably feel sad, mad, bad—or a mixture of all three. When it happens, here are some things you can do: 1. Apologize to the people you've hurt; 2. Fix the things you've messed up or broken; 3. Don't make the same mistake again; 4. Ask God for His forgiveness (which, by the way, He will give to you instantly); 5. Forgive yourself; and 6. Get busy doing something you can be proud of.

Big Idea for Kids

You can make it right . . . if you think you can! If you've made a mistake, apologize. If you've broken something, fix it. If you've hurt someone's feelings, apologize. If you failed at something, try again. There is always something you can do to make things better . . . so do it!

If you can't forgive yourself,
you're saying Christ didn't do enough.
Anonymous

Big Idea for Parents

When You Make a Mistake, Admit It: No parent is perfect, not even you. Consequently, you will make mistakes from time to time (and yes, you might even lose your temper). When you make a mistake, apologize to the offended party, especially if that party is related to you by birth.

Today's Prayer

Dear Lord, I have made mistakes,
and You have forgiven me.
Thank You for Your forgiveness.
When I am not perfect,
help other people to forgive me,
and help me forgive myself.
Amen

Forgiving Family

Whoever brings trouble with his family will be left with nothing but the wind.

Proverbs 11:29 ICB

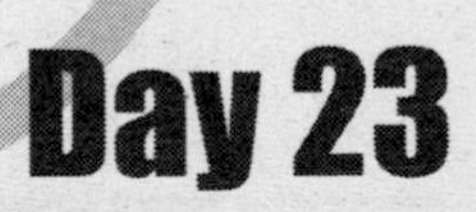

Day 23

Sometimes, it's easy to become angry with the people we love most, and sometimes it's hard to forgive them. After all, we know that our family will still love us no matter how angry we become. But while it's easy to become angry at home, it's usually wrong.

The next time you're tempted to stay angry at a brother, or a sister, or a parent, remember that these are the people who love you more than anybody else! Then, calm down, and forgive them . . . NOW! Because peace is always beautiful, especially when it's peace at your house.

Big Idea for Kids

Since you love your family . . . let them know it by the things you say and the things you do. And, never take your family members for granted; they deserve your very best treatment!

There is always room for more loving forgiveness within our homes.
James Dobson

Big Idea for Parents

You may become angry, but . . . Of course, you will experience times when you feel anger toward family members, but your love for them should never be in question. Our love for our families must never be turned on and off like the garden hose; it should, instead, flow like a mighty river, too deep to touch bottom and too strong to stop.

Today's Prayer

Dear Lord, You have given me
a wonderful gift: a loving family.
Today and every day, let me show
my family that I love them by
the words that I speak and
way that I behave.
Amen

Because It's The Right Thing to Do

Those who are pure in their thinking
are happy, because they will be with God.

Matthew 5:8 NCV

Day 24

God gave you something called a conscience: it's that little feeling that tells you whether something is right or wrong. Your conscience will usually tell you what to do and when to do it. Trust that feeling.

If you stop to listen to your conscience, it won't be as hard for you to forgive people. Why? Because forgiving other people is the right thing to do. And, it's what God wants you to do. And it's what your conscience tells you to do. So what are you waiting for?

Big Idea for Kids

That little voice inside your head . . . is called your conscience. Listen to it; it's usually right!

> To go against one's conscience is
> neither safe nor right. Here I stand.
> I cannot do otherwise.
>
> Martin Luther

Big Idea for Parents

Sometimes, the little voice that we hear in our heads can be the echoes of our own parents' voices . . . and now that we're parents ourselves, we're the ones whose words will echo down through the hearts and minds of future generations. It's a big responsibility, but with God's help, we're up to the challenge.

Today's Prayer

Dear God, You've given me a conscience
that tells me right from wrong.
Let me trust my conscience, and let me
live according to Your teachings,
not just for today, but forever.
Amen

Understanding the Other Person

If it costs everything you have,
get understanding.
Proverbs 4:7 NCV

There's an old saying that goes something like this: "Try to put yourself in the other person's shoes." It means that the more you understand somebody, the easier it is to forgive that person.

When you become angry with someone, try putting yourself in the other person's shoes. When you do, perhaps you'll be a little bit more understanding—and a little bit quicker to forgive.

Big Idea for Kids

Respecting all kinds of people: Make sure that you show proper respect for everyone, even if that person happens to be different from you. It's easy to make fun of people who seem different . . . but it's wrong.

The old saying is true:
People don't care what we know
until they know we care.
Rick Warren

Big Idea for Parents

It starts with you: Remember that kindness, dignity, and respect for others begin at the head of the household and work their way down from there. And our kids are always watching!

Today's Prayer

Dear Lord, let me be an understanding person, especially to my family and friends. Let me be kind to those who need my encouragement and let me be a helpful, generous Christian today and every day.

Amen

The Best Time to Forgive

So when you offer your gift to God
at the altar, and you remember that your
brother or sister has something against you,
leave your gift there at the altar.
Go and make peace with that person,
and then come and offer your gift.

Matthew 5:23-24 NCV

Day 26

When is the best time to forgive somebody? Well, as the old saying goes, there's no time like the present. So if you have somebody you need to forgive, why not forgive that person today?

Forgiving other people is one of the ways that we make ourselves feel better. So if you're still angry about something that somebody did, forgive that person right now. There is no better time.

Big Idea for Kids

The time to forgive is now! God wants you to forgive people now, not later. Why? Because God knows that it's the right thing to do. And, of course, God wants you to be happy, not angry. God knows what's best for you, so if you have somebody you need to forgive, do it now.

If you're going to forgive somebody,
why wait?
Marie T. Freeman

Big Idea for Parents

Bearing a grudge = bearing a burden: You know what a heavy burden it can be to bear a grudge against another person; make sure that your child knows, too!

Today's Prayer

Dear Lord, whenever I am angry,
give me a forgiving heart. And help me
remember that the best day
to forgive somebody is this one.
Amen

When People Aren't Nice

Whoever forgives someone's sin
makes a friend . . . .
Proverbs 17:9 NCV

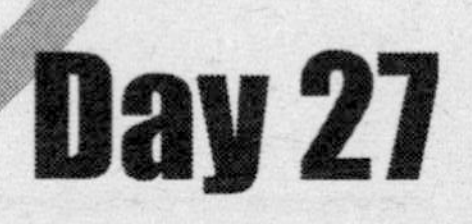

Face it: sometimes people aren't nice. And when other people are unkind to you, or they are unkind to someone you love, you may be tempted to strike out in anger. Don't do it! Instead, remember that God corrects other people's behaviors in His own way, and He probably doesn't need your help. And remember that God has commanded you to forgive other people, just as you seek forgiveness from others when you misbehave.

So, when other people aren't nice, forgive them as quickly as you can. And leave the rest up to God.

Big Idea for Kids

Stand up and be counted! Do you know children who say or do cruel things to other kids? If so, don't join in! Instead, stand up for those who need your help. It's the right thing to do.

We are all fallen creatures
and all very hard to live with.
C. S. Lewis

Big Idea for Parents

Let's face it: even the most angelic children can do things that are unfair or unkind. When we observe such behavior in our own children, we must be understanding, but firm. We live in a world where misbehavior is tolerated and, in many cases, glorified. But inside the walls of our own homes, misbehavior should not be ignored; it should be corrected by loving, courageous parents.

Today's Prayer

Dear Lord, sometimes it's very hard
to forgive those who have hurt me,
but with Your help, I can forgive them.
Help me to bring forgiveness into
my heart so that I can forgive others
just as You have already forgiven me.
Amen

Because God Forgives Us

My whole being, praise the Lord
and do not forget all his kindnesses.
He forgives all my sins.

Psalm 103:2-3 NCV

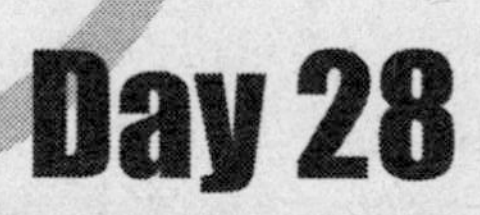

How often does God forgive us? More times than we can count! And that, by the way, is exactly how many times that God expects us to forgive other people—more times than we care to count.

Of this you can be sure: God won't ever get tired of forgiving you. And, because He has forgiven you, He doesn't want you to get tired of forgiving other people . . . ever!

Big Idea for Kids

God's love is forever! One of the most important lessons that you can ever learn is to trust God for everything. He loves you forever, and He will never let you down!

God forgives me and stands with
arms open wide to welcome me home.
Sheila Walsh

Big Idea for Parents

Reminder to moms and dads: There are many ways to say, "I love you." Find them. Put love notes in lunch pails and on pillows; hug relentlessly; laugh and play with abandon.

Today's Prayer

Dear God, the Bible teaches me that Your love lasts forever. Thank You, God, for Your love. Let me trust Your promises, and let me live according to Your teachings, not just for today, but forever.

Amen

Pray About It!

Then if my people, who are called by my name, are sorry for what they have done, if they pray and obey me and stop their evil ways, I will hear them from heaven. I will forgive their sin, and I will heal their land.

2 Chronicles 7:14 NCV

If you are upset, pray about it. If there is person you don't like, pray for a forgiving heart. If there is something you're worried about, ask God to comfort you. And as you pray more, you'll discover that God is always near and that He's always ready to hear from you. So don't worry about things; pray about them. God is waiting . . . and listening!

Big Idea for Kids

Pray early and often: One way to make sure that your heart is in tune with God is to pray often. The more you talk to God, the more He will talk to you.

> I firmly believe a great many prayers are not answered because we are not willing to forgive someone.
>
> D. L. Moody

Big Idea for Parents

Be a prayerful parent: God is listening, and your children are watching.

Today's Prayer

Dear Lord, whether I am feeling good
or bad, whether I am happy
or sad, I will pray.
You always hear my prayers, God;
let me always pray them!
Amen

Imitating Jesus

This is what you were called to do,
because Christ suffered for you
and gave you an example to follow.
So you should do as he did.
1 Peter 2:21 NCV

Day 30

If you're not certain whether something is right or wrong, ask yourself a simple question: "How would Jesus behave if He were here?" The answer to that question will tell you what to do.

Jesus was perfect, but we are not. Still, we must try as hard as we can to be like Him. When we do, we will love others, just like Christ loves us.

Big Idea for Kids

Someone very near you may need a helping hand or a kind word, so keep your eyes open, and look for people who need your help, whether at home, at church, or at school.

If we want to do something for God,
now is the time.
Vance Havner

Big Idea for Parents

Preach, teach, and reach . . . out!: When it comes to teaching our children how to become faithful servants of Christ, our sermons are not as important as our service. Charity should start at home—with parents—and work its way down the family tree from there.

Today's Prayer

Lord, when I am uncertain what to do, let me look to Jesus as my example. Let me do my best to behave like Jesus would behave if He were in my place. Thank You, Lord, for a perfect example of the perfect way to behave; that example is Your Son.

Amen

For God So Loved the World

For God loved the world in this way:
He gave His only Son, so that everyone
who believes in Him will not perish
but have eternal life.

John 3:16 Holman CSB

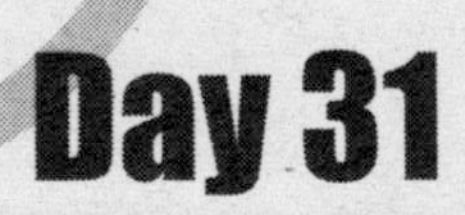

How much does God love you? He loves you so much that He sent His Son Jesus to come to this earth for you! And, when you accept Jesus into your heart, God gives you a gift that is more precious than gold: that gift is called "eternal life," which means that you will live forever with God in heaven!

God's love is bigger and more powerful than anybody can imagine, but it is very real. So do yourself a favor right now: accept God's love with open arms and welcome His Son Jesus into your heart. When you do, your life will be changed today, tomorrow, and forever.

Big Idea for Kids

What a friend you have in Jesus: Jesus loves you, and He offers you eternal life with Him in heaven. Welcome Him into your heart. Now!

> If God had a refrigerator,
> your picture would be on it.
>
> Max Lucado

Big Idea for Parents

The Truth with a capital "T": Hannah Whitall Smith wrote, "The crucial question for each of us is this: What do you think of Jesus, and do you yet have a personal acquaintance with Him?" As parents, we must also ask ourselves another question: do our children know what we think about Jesus? And if not, why not?

Today's Prayer

Dear Lord, thank You for Your Son.
Jesus loves me and He shares so much
with me. Let me share His love
with others so that through me,
they can understand what
it means to follow Him.
Amen

Bible Verses to Remember

The Lord is my shepherd;
I shall not want. He makes me
to lie down in green pastures;
He leads me beside the still waters.
He restores my soul.

Psalm 23:1-3 NKJV

Yes, if you forgive others for
the things they do wrong,
then your Father in heaven
will also forgive you for
the things you do wrong.

Matthew 6:14 ICB

Whoever does not love does not know God, because God is love.

1 John 4:8 ICB

Do to others what you want them to do to you.

Matthew 7:12 NCV

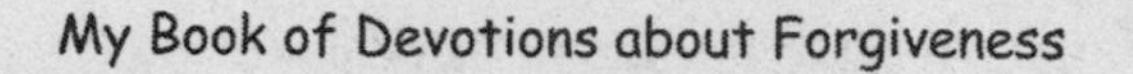

Now these three remain:
faith, hope, and love.
But the greatest of these is love.

1 Corinthians 13:13 Holman CSB

Draw near to God, and He will draw near to you.

James 4:8 Holman CSB

We love Him because He first loved us.

1 John 4:19 NKJV

**This is the day the LORD has made;
we will rejoice and be glad in it.**

Psalm 118:24 NKJV

Jesus said to him,
"You shall love the Lord your God with all your heart, with all your soul, and with all your mind. This is the first and great commandment.
And the second is like it:
'You shall love your neighbor as yourself.'"

Matthew 22:37-39 NKJV

I am able to do all things through Him who strengthens me.

Philippians 4:13 Holman CSB

Let not your heart be troubled;
you believe in God,
believe also in Me.

John 14:1 NKJV

Be still, and know that I am God . . . .

Psalm 46:10 KJV

Blessings crown the head of the righteous . . . .

Proverbs 10:6 NIV

Rejoice in the Lord always; again I will say, rejoice!

Philippians 4:4 NASB

A good name is to be chosen over great wealth.

Proverbs 22:1 Holman CSB

God loves a cheerful giver.

2 Corinthians 9:7 NIV

Therefore, if anyone is in Christ,
he is a new creation;
the old has gone, the new has come!

2 Corinthians 5:17 NIV